Dear

Have a happy Christmas
1998, and a Great
Year in 1999!

THE FÆRIE KINGDOM

Saint Francis and Saint Benedight,
Bless this house from wicked wight;
From the night-mare and the goblin
That is hight Goodfellow Robin;
Keep it from all evil spirits,
Fairies, weasels, rats and ferrets:
From curfew time,
To the next prime.

William Cartwright, 1611–43

THE FÆRIE
KINGDOM

Celia Haddon

SIMON & SCHUSTER

A VIACOM COMPANY

First published in Great Britain by Simon & Schuster Ltd, 1998
A Viacom company

Copyright © Celia Haddon, 1998
Illustrations copyright © as acknowledged on page 106

1   3   5   7   9   10   8   6   4   2

Simon & Schuster Ltd
West Garden Place
Kendal Street
London W2 2AQ

Simon & Schuster Australia
Sydney

A CIP catalogue record for this book is available
from the British Library
Colour reproduction by Pica Colour Separation, Singapore
Printed In Hong Kong by Midas Printing Ltd
Designed by Peter Ward

ISBN 0-684-84066-9

CONTENTS

[v]

PREFACE

NTIL RECENTLY IN THIS CENTURY, FÆRIES WERE considered a suitable subject only for children's books. Today, however, there has been an explosion of adult interest in the færie kingdom. A new genre of books, so-called færie science fiction, with its elves, gnomes and goblins, has swept the English-speaking world. In Hollywood a new interest has been found in færie film. Færies flourish on the Internet, where there are role-playing færie sites, færie encyclopaedias, færie spells and traders selling færie sundries. Elsewhere færie shamans and færie queens offer rituals, magic and counselling. Færie culture is to be found all over the English-speaking world.

The færie heritage of English-speaking peoples goes back hundreds of years to the wilder areas of the British Isles, including but not entirely synonymous with the Celtic parts — Ireland, Wales, the Highlands of Scotland, the Scottish borders, the North Country, Cornwall and the West Country. This book outlines the færie themes common to this heritage — themes which have now spread to America, Australia and New Zealand.

Opposite: Detail of *The Reconciliation of Oberon and Titania*, Sir Joseph Noel Paton (1821–1901)

In Europe, each country had slightly different (though generally similar) færie populations: the leshy of the Baltic countries, the water nixies of Germany, Scandinavian nisses, the trolls of Iceland, to name but a few. Common to all Europe was a belief in a race of non-human mostly unseen people who live alongside us.

Enemies threatened these beliefs from early times. One enemy was the Christian authorities, which, at various times in history, declared that a belief in færies is a belief in devils. People were tortured and burned for having seen færies. Færie beliefs, however, persisted. For a time in medieval Europe they even became fashionable in the literature of the French and British courts. The legends of King Arthur and his knights include stories of the færie kingdom. (Arthurian stories are best read in their entirety and so I have not included them in this short book.) In England, it was at the time of Elizabeth I that færies flourished most. Shakespeare and other poets and playwrights, such as Michael Drayton and Robert Herrick, chose them as the subject for some of their best work. Yet færies came

Above: *A Midsummer Night's Dream*, Sir Joseph Noel Paton

under threat again when James I, successor to Elizabeth I, declared that færies were illusions created by the devil.

From the mouths of those prosecuted for believing in færies, in witchcraft trials, came some of the traditional stories of færies. Issobel Gowdie, a reputed Scottish witch, for instance, confessed that the devil made elf arrowheads which were then given needles by elves. The belief that flint arrowheads were fæated weapons was repeated by this poor soul under torture. 'We have now bow to shoot with, but spang them from the nails of our thumbs,' she said.

Fæated tales followed the early immigrants in the seventeenth century to the New World, though in the witch-hunting culture of New England it would have been unwise to retell stories of pucks and goblins and fæated queens. For several generations there the fæated kingdom had to remain not just an unseen world, but one unspoken-of too.

Native Americans, of course, had their own beliefs. The Algonquin in Canada and the north-eastern United States believed in the manitou, a kind of fæated folk with antlers on their foreheads. The Passamaquoddy tribe believed in small ugly fæated called the nagum-wasuck. Likewise in Australia the Aborigines had their own version of fæated — mimis, which lived in rock crevices and were so thin they could be blown away by the wind. But immigrants arriving from Britain in Australia, from the eighteenth century onwards, brought their own fæated beliefs with them, enthusiastically naming several Fairy Mountains, Fairy Meadows and Meads, Fairy Dells and even a Fairy Island.

The eighteenth century, when fæated beliefs spread round the world, was also the age of the educated élite, whose views threatened færie beliefs. In the nursery, boys might hear færie stories from the servants, but at school their education was strictly classical. Latin and Greek were the mark of educated people: schools taught more about nymphs, satyrs and centaurs than about their own native færies, and writers and poets peopled their literary landscapes with a classical mythology. Most educated people had little time for færies. Those that did considered færies attractive inventions, rather than beings worthy of respect. Færies 'belong to the bloom of fancy, a thing generally too frail and beautiful to withstand the rude handling of time,' wrote the essayist Charles Lamb, from whom one might have expected better.

The poet William Blake, who believed in and even saw færies, was very much the exception. Other interest in færies came from antiquarians and eccentrics such as John Aubrey and George Waldron in the Isle of Man. They began to write down the beliefs still held in the countryside. It is clear that both were fascinated by such stories and probably either partly or wholly believed them. A later generation, led by Sir Walter Scott, started consistently collecting first the old ballads and then the general body of færie beliefs. They turned to the remoter areas of the British Isles, still untouched by the Industrial Revolution, which displaced many people from their folk origins. In the Highlands of Scotland, the Devon countryside and Ireland, people still believed in the unseen world and took precautions to protect themselves against it.

For this anthology I have chosen many passages from the early antiquarians and these folklore collectors, for their writings are the most reliable accounts of the færie kingdom. At that time færie stories

in their hundreds were also being collected all over Europe. But I have concentrated only on those from Britain and Ireland. (It is not possible in this small book to do justice either to the stories of the rest of Europe or those of the native American and Aboriginal cultures.) It is these stories that have gone round the globe with the English language.

The best-known færie tales from other European countries are those collected by two brothers, Jacob and Wilhelm Grimm, German

Above: *A Glimpse of the Fairies*, Charles Hutton Lear (1818–1903)

folklorists. Their *Household Tales*, first published in English in the nineteenth century, became a children's favourite. Ironically this was perhaps the greatest disaster that has befallen the unseen kingdom. For the popularity of Grimms' stories inspired writers in the nineteenth and twentieth centuries to write about færies for children, and in doing so they ignored the authentic færies and made the færie kingdom into

Above: *There Sleeps Titania*, John Simmons (1823–76)

a twee world of pretty harmless little beings. The term 'fairy story' became synonymous with fiction. In the seventeenth century, the færies had been feared as devils, even loathed, but at least were given some stature. As the saccharine little beings of Victorian books they gained no respect. I use the word 'færie', rather than 'fairy', to get away from this image of twee wee folk.

From the 1790s to the 1890s, fairy painting became a recognized genre. Victorian painters, unlike children's authors, recognized the power and mystery of færies. Among the best-known Victorian painters were two Celts, Daniel Maclise and Sir Joseph Noel Paton. Of Paton it was said that his paintings were 'so full of what we may call the moonlit atmosphere of Færie, that the artist at once took first rank in this line of art.' Paton's færies are the true thing – beings of mystery, sometimes beautiful, often erotic, sometimes terrifying. Equally impressive are the supernatural beings painted by John Anster Fitzgerald, Richard Dadd and the illustrators Richard Doyle and George Cruikshank. It is mainly paintings by these artists that illustrate this book.

It was John Ronald Tolkein who rescued færies from children's books. He restored them to their rightful place, a realm of mystery, power and danger. As an expert on Anglo-Saxon and medieval literature he would have known many of the extracts in this book. With his saga *The Lord of the Rings*, published in the 1950s, færie subjects became a matter for adults again.

But are there really færies? I have seen one, but I was only four years old and I do not know if it was really there. I also have known

several people, including some of my relatives, who saw færies. I do not believe they lied in telling of such sightings.

Today people still report færie appearances in the traditional areas of Britain. And sightings of these types of færies have also been reported in America, Canada and Australia, suggesting that in an unseen world of færies, location may be a matter of indifference to some of the good people. There is a story that a mermaid, a sea færie, once followed a ship all the way from Ireland to America; another describes how an Irish banshee, which foretold death for the O'Grady family, followed them to Canada. Do færies follow people because in some way they have a symbiotic relationship with human society?

It is the surprising consistency of the tales that suggests there may be truth in færie legend. In literature from medieval times to this century, traditional themes recur. The tales in this book typically show that they are not the recent inventions of fiction writers and that from century to century the unseen world has indeed been briefly glimpsed.

Those who favour a world of dull facts will be sure that there are no færies, just as there are no angels, no devils, no human souls and no God. Yet there is more to the world than can be seen, measured and reduced to hard statistics. Come with me and see — into the unseen and living færie kingdom.

Opposite: Detail of *Midsummer Eve*, Edward Robert Hughes (1851–1914)

CHAPTER ONE

INTRODUCTION TO THE FÆRIE KINGDOM

THE UNSEEN WORLD OF FÆRIES CANNOT BE explored, mapped or accurately described like some hitherto unknown country, for we see it only in glimpses, at the margins of our sight, or sense it so briefly that we cannot be sure it is really there. And yet the sights and sounds of that strange country are nevertheless seen and heard by some human beings.

Who or what are færies? Some histories say they are the spirits of the dead; others claim they are fallen angels; still others fear them as devils. One old tradition holds that they are a third race of spiritual beings, somewhere between angels and mankind. As well as the broad highway to hell, and the narrow steep road to heaven, there is a third path — the way to færie land, out of normal human time, out of normal human space and out of normal human morality. Are they from an alternative universe? Or a race once plentiful in the wild places of the natural earth, now dwindling as concrete spreads over the natural countryside?

Most agree that the path to færie land is a perilous one, not to

Opposite: Detail of *The Release of Ariel*, John Anster Fitzgerald (1832–1906)

be trodden lightly, and that the consequences of being led by færies may be tragic. If we fall under their enchantment we may lose all – our families, our homes and perhaps even our souls to the strange glamour of the færie kingdom.

The Reverend Robert Kirk, a seventeenth-century authority on the unseen world, may have incurred the enmity of the færie folk by writing a book about them, as we shall see in Chapter Four. Even those who merely walk in places where færies may be found would do well to remember to call these beings 'good neighbours', 'men of peace', 'good folk', not because they are good, but for fear of their anger. Careless or offensive talk may cost human lives.

Any research into the færie kingdom must start with the old texts. For there is a body of knowledge of the unseen world, built up by historians, folklorists and true believers, to be found in old tales still told to the trustworthy, and in the writings and paintings of those who tried to see through the veil that divides the human world from the færie one.

Opposite: *Asleep in the Moonlight*, Richard Doyle (1824–83)

THE FÆRIES OF IRELAND

ROM THE EARLIEST AGES the world has believed in the existence of a race midway between the angel and man, gifted with the power to exercise a strange mysterious influence over human destiny . . . The Irish called them the Sidhe, or spirit-race . . . Their country is the Tirna-oge, the land of perpetual youth, where they live a life of joy and beauty, never knowing disease or death, which is not to come on them till the judgement day, when they are fated to pass into annihilation, to perish utterly and be seen no more. They can assume any form and they make horses out of bits of straw on which they ride over the country, and to Scotland and back . . . Underneath the lakes, and deep down in the heart of the hills, they have their fairy palaces of pearl and gold, where they live in splendour and luxury, with music and song and dancing and laughter and all joyous things as befits the gods of the earth. If our eyes were touched by a fairy salve we could see them dancing on the hill in the moonlight. They are served on vessels of gold, and each fairy chief, to mark his rank, wears a circlet of gold round his head. The Sidhe race were once angels in heaven, but were banished as a punishment for their pride. Some fell to earth, others were cast into the sea, while many were seized by demons and carried down to hell, whence they issue as evil spirits, to tempt men to destruction under various disguises; chiefly, however, as beautiful young maidens, endowed with the power of song and gifted with the most enchanting wiles.

Lady Wilde, *Ancient Legends, Mystic Charms and Superstitions of Ireland,* 1887

THE FÆRIES OF SCOTLAND

HESE *Siths*, or Fairies, they call *Sleagh Maith*, or the Good People, it would seem, to prevent the dint of their ill attempts (for the Irish use to bless all they fear harm of); and are said to be of a middle nature betwixt man and angel, as were dæmons thought to be of old; of intelligent studious spirits, and light changeable bodies (like those called astral), somewhat of the nature of a condensed cloud, and best seen in twilight. These bodies be so pliable thorough the subtlety of the spirits that agitate them, that they can make them appear or disappear at pleasure. Some have bodies or vehicles so spungious, thin and desiccate, that they are fed by only sucking into some fine spirituous liquors, that pierce like pure air and oil: others feed more gross on the foyson [harvest] or substance of corns and liquors, or corn itself that grows on the surface of the earth, which these fairies steal away, partly invisible, partly preying on the grain, as do crows and mice; wherefore in this same age, they are some times heard to bake bread, strike hammers, and do such like services within the little hillocks they most haunt: some whereof of old, before the gospel

dispelled paganism, and in some barbarous places as yet, enter houses after all are at rest, and set the kitchens in order, cleansing all the vessels. Such drags go under the name of brownies . . . Their bodies of congealed air are some times carried aloft, other whiles grovel in different shapes, and enter into any cranny or cleft of the earth where air enters, to their ordinary dwellings; the earth being full of cavities and cells . . . We then (the more terrestrial kind have now so numerously planted all countries) do labour for that abstruse people, as well as for ourselves. Albeit, when several countries were uninhabited by us, these had their easy tillage above ground, as we now. The print of those furrows do yet remain to be seen on the shoulders of very high hills, which was done when the champayn [cultivated] ground was wood and forest.

Robert Kirk, *The Secret Commonwealth*, 1691

Opposite: Detail of *Spirit of the Night*, John Atkinson Grimshaw (1863–93)

THE PATH TO FÆRIE

Light down, light down, now True Thomas,
And lean your head upon my knee;
Abide and rest a little space,
And I will show you ferlies three.

Above: *Thomas the Rhymer*, Sir Joseph Noel Paton

O see ye not yon narrow road,
So thick beset with thorns and briers?
That is the path of righteousness,
Tho' after it but few enquires.

And see ye not that braid braid road,
That lies across that lily leven?
That is the path of wickedness,
Tho' some call it the road to heaven.

And see not ye that bonny road,
That winds about the fernie brae?
That is the road to fair Elfland,
Where thou and I this night maun gae . . .

O they rade on, and farther on,
And they waded thro' rivers aboon the knee,
And they saw neither sun nor moon,
But they heard the roaring of the sea.

It was mirk mirk night, and there was nae stern light,
And they waded thro' red blude to the knee;
For a' the blude that's shed on earth
Rins thro' the springs o' that countrie.

'Thomas the Rhymer', traditional Scottish and North Country ballad

A FÆRY SPEAKS

What I am, I must not show –
What I am thou couldst not know –
Something betwixt heaven and hell –
Something that neither stood nor fell –
Something that through thy wit or will
May work thee good – may work thee ill.

Above: *Come unto these Yellow Sands*, Richard Dadd (1819–87)

[20]

Neither substance quite, nor shadow,
Haunting lonely moor and meadow,
Dancing by the haunted spring,
Riding on the whirlwind's wing;
Aping in fantastic fashion
Every change of human passion,
While o'er our frozen minds they pass,
Like shadows from the mirror'd glass.
Wayward, fickle, is our mood,
Hovering betwixt bad and good,
Happier than brief-dated man,
Living ten times o'er his span;
Far less happy, for we have
Help nor hope beyond the grave!
Man awakes to joy or sorrow;
Ours the sleep that knows no morrow.
This is all that I can show —
This is all that thou may'st know.

Sir Walter Scott, *The Monastery*, 1820

WEST OF ENGLAND PIXIES

HE PIXIES ARE CERTAINLY a distinct race from the fairies; since, to this hour, the elders amongst the more knowing peasantry of Devon will invariably tell you (if you ask them what pixies really may be) that these

Above: *The Captive Robin*, John Anster Fitzgerald

native spirits are the souls of infants, who were so unhappy as to die before they had received the Christian rite of baptism. These tiny elves are said to delight in solitary places, to love pleasant hills and pathless woods; or to disport themselves on the margins of rivers and mountain streams . . . These dainty beings, though represented as of exceeding beauty in their higher or aristocratic order, are nevertheless, in some instances, of strange, uncouth and fantastic figure and visage: though such natural deformity need give them very little uneasiness, since they are traditionally averred to possess the power of assuming various shapes at will . . . But whatever changes the outward figure of fairies may undergo, they are, amongst themselves, as constant in their fashions as a Turk; their dress never varies, it is always green.

Mrs Bray, *Traditions, Legends, Superstitions, and Sketches of Devonshire*, 1838

THE FÆRIES OF WALES

AIRIES WERE NOT ALL OF the same species, but were almost invariably associated with hilly districts. They varied according to the districts to which they belonged . . . In some districts the fairies are described as diminutive beings with strong thieving propensities, who used to live in summer among the bracken on the mountains, and in winter among the heather and gorse. These used to frequent fairs, and steal the farmers' money from their pockets, placing in their stead the coins of the fairies, which counterfeited the ordinary money; but when they were paid for anything that had been bought, they would vanish in the seller's pocket. In other districts they were described as somewhat bigger and stronger people; but these were also of a thieving disposition, and would lurk about people's houses, watching their opportunity to steal the butter and cheese from the dairy. They would also loiter about the cow yards, and would sometimes milk the cows and goats so dry that there would be no milk whatever left for many a morning. But the greatest sport this species had was in stealing unchristened babies, and placing their own puny and peevish offspring in their place . . . There is still another species very unlike the foregoing in disposition and nature. Not only did they far surpass them in beauty and comeliness, but they also treated mortals with honesty and kindness. Their whole nature was brimful of joy and merriment; they were hardly ever seen except at some harmless fun. They could be seen on clear moonlight nights singing and carolling lightheartedly on the fair meadows and green hillslopes, or tripping lightly on the tips of the bulrushes as they danced in the valley; and they could be seen following vigorously in the hunt on their gray horses, for this species was truly opulent, having servants and horses of the finest sort. Though they were said to be spiritual and immortal beings, they nevertheless ate and drank, married and begat children, just like human beings . . .

D. E. Jenkins, *Bedd Gelert: Its Faces, Fairies and Folklore*, 1899

THE WIND ON THE HILLS

Go not to the hills of Erinn
When the night winds are about,
Put up your bar and shutter,
And so keep the danger out.

Above: *Fairies' Whirl*, Arthur John Black (1855–1936)

For the good-folk whirl within it,
And they pull you by the hand,
And they push you on the shoulder,
Till you move to their command.

And lo! you have forgotten
What you have known of tears,
And you will not remember
That the world goes full of years;

Above: *'Who Killed Cock Robin?'*, John Anster Fitzgerald

A year there is a lifetime,
And a second but a day,
And an older world will meet you
Each morn you come away.

Your wife grows old with weeping,
And your children one by one
Grow grey with nights of watching,
Before your dance is done.

And it will chance some morning
You will come home no more;
Your wife sees but a withered leaf
In the wind about the door . . .

Dora Sigerson Shorter, 1866–1918

CHAPTER TWO

THE WORLD OF FÆRIES

HE UNSEEN WORLD OF FÆRIES IS A KINGDOM, not a republic. 'They are said to have aristocratical rulers and laws,' reported the Reverend Robert Kirk three hundred years ago. A queen and king rule their færie subjects and it is the queen who is seen more often by human beings. Shakespeare called the king Oberon and the queen Titania in *A Midsummer Night's Dream*; the queen is also known as Mab.

The court has its palace, usually below ground in a hillock or a cave, often near a hawthorn tree. Sometimes the noise of laughter and feasting, glimpses of light or sounds of music can be heard by passers-by. The færies come out on moonlit nights to dance on the greensward. Færie rings — circles of darker green grass seen on pasture land, sometimes with toadstools or mushrooms — mark their dancing ground. Færies also hold fairs and markets in country places.

Færies may be seen above ground moving from one palace to another, hunting deer or smaller game, or going to war against færie rivals. This is the færie rade, a procession with steeds — sometimes horses, sometimes smaller animals — tinkling with silver bells and accompanied by the sound of music or chanting. Occasionally the rade

Opposite: *The Quarrel of Oberon and Titania*, Sir Joseph Noel Paton

is airborne. For færies can fly or, more accurately, levitate. Victorian paintings often show færies with butterfly wings and some færies in literature seem to have these. But the older stories make it clear that færies can whirl in the air without them.

The size of færies varies. West-of-England fairies seem to be smaller than human beings — sometimes very small indeed. Yet the Scottish færie queen who, as we have seen, lured away Thomas the Rhymer was human in size. Since færies can change their shape, it is likely that they can change their size at will too. Perhaps the spell they cast upon us makes us see them either small or large, as they choose.

Færies also have at their command magic. They can ill wish humans and cause disease on animals or crops; or they can bless with good luck or grant wishes. Unlike sorcerers, færies are not preoccupied with magic, but they use it for their own ends to reward or punish humans, as those who venture on færy ground may discover.

FÆRIES OR DEVILS?

SOME PUT OUR FAIRIES INTO this rank (of terrestrial devils), which have been in former times adored with much superstition, with sweeping their houses and setting of a pail of clean water, good victuals and the like, and then they should not be pinched but find money in their shoes, and be fortunate in their enterprises. These are they that dance on heaths and greens, . . . and . . . leave that green circle which we

Above: *Triumphal March of the Elf King*, Richard Doyle

commonly find in plain fields, which others hold to proceed from a
meteor falling, or some accidental rankness of the ground, so nature
sports herself; they are sometimes seen by old women and children
. . . Giraldius Cambrensis gives instance in a monk of Wales that was
so deluded. Paracelsus reckons up many places in Germany where
they do usually walk in little coats, some two feet long. A bigger kind
there is of them called with us hobgoblins and Robin Goodfellows,
that would in those superstitious times grind corn for a mess of
milk, cut wood or do any matter of drudgery work . . . And so

Above: *The Haunted Park*, Richard Doyle

likewise those . . . that walk about midnight on great heaths and desert places, which (saith Lavater) draw men out of the way, and lead them all night a by-way, or quite bar them of their way. These have several names in several places; we commonly call them Pucks.

Robert Burton, *Anatomy of Melancholy*, 1651

THE FÆRIES

Come follow, follow me,
You fairy elves that be;
And circle round this green,
Come follow me, your Queen.
Hand in hand let's dance a round,
For this place is fairy ground.

When mortals are at rest,
And snorting in their nest,
Unheard, or unespied
Through keyholes we do glide:
Over tables, stools and shelves,
We trip it with our fairy elves.

And if the house be fowl,
Or platter, dish, or bowl,
Upstairs we nimbly creep,
And find the sluts asleep;
Then we pinch their arms and thighs,
None escapes, nor none espies.

But if the house be swept,
And from uncleanness kept,
We praise the house and maid,
For surely she is paid:
For we do use before we go
To drop a tester in her shoe . . .

Over the tender grass
So lightly we can pass,
The young and tender stalk
Ne'er bows whereon we walk,
Nor in the morning dew to seen,
Over night where we have been . . .

Anonymous English poem, seventeenth century

FÆRIE MUSIC

THEIR LOVE OF DANCING is not unaccompanied with that of music, though it is often of a nature somewhat different to those sounds which human ears are apt to consider harmonious. In Devonshire, that unlucky omen, the cricket's cry, is to them as animating and as well timed as the piercing notes of the fife, or the dulcet melody of rebec or flute, to mortals. The frogs sing their double bass, and the screech owl is to them like an aged and favoured minstrel piping in hall.

Above: *There is Sweet Music Here*, Charles Robinson (1870–1937)

Above: *The Concert*, John Anster Fitzgerald

The grasshopper, too, chirps with his merry note in the concert, and the humming bee plays 'his hautbois' to their tripping on the green; as the small stream, on whose banks they hold their sports, seems to share their hilarity, and talks and dances as well as they in emulation of the revelry; whilst it shows through its crystal waters a gravelly bed as bright as burnished gold, the jewel-house of fairy land; or else the pretty stream lies sparkling in the moonbeam, for no hour is so dear to pixy revels as that in which man sleeps, and the queen of night, who loves not his mortal gaze, becomes a watcher. It is under the cold and chaste light of her beams or amidst the silent shadows of the dark rocks, where that light never penetrates, that on the moor the elfin king of the pixy race holds his high court of sovereignty and council.

Mrs Bray, *Traditions, Legends, Superstitions, and Sketches of Devonshire*, 1838

QUEEN MAB

O, then I see Queen Mab hath been with you.
She is the fairies' midwife, and she comes
In shape no bigger than an agate stone
On the forefinger of an alderman,
Drawn with a team of little atomies

Athwart men's noses as they lie asleep;
Her wagon-spokes made of long spinners' legs,
The cover of the wings of grasshoppers,
The traces of the smallest spider's web,
The collars of the moonshine's watery beams,
Her whip of cricket's bone, the lash of film,
Her wagoner a small grey-coated gnat,
Not half so big as a round little worm

Above: *Queen Mab*, Henry Maynell Rheam (1859–1920)

Pricked from the lazy finger of a maid;
Her chariot is an empty hazel nut
Made by the joiner squirrel or old grub,
Time out o' mind the fairies' coach-makers.
And in this state she gallops night by night
Through lovers' brains, and then they dream of love;
O'er courtiers' knees, that dream on court'sies straight;
O'er lawyers' fingers, who straight dream of fees;
O'er ladies' lips, who straight on kisses dream
Which oft the angry Mab with blisters plagues,
Because their breaths with sweetmeats tainted are:
Sometimes she gallops o'er a courtier's nose,
And then dreams he of smelling out a suit;
And sometimes comes she with a tithe-pig's tail
Tickling a parson's nose as a' lies asleep,
Then dreams he of another benefice . . .
                         This is that very Mab
That plaits the manes of horses in the night,
And bakes the elf-locks in foul sluttish hairs
Which once untangled much misfortune bodes.

William Shakespeare, *Romeo and Juliet*, 1596

THE FÆRY RADE

 YOUNG SAILOR ... coming off a long voyage, tho' it was late at night, chose to land rather than lie another night in the vessel: being permitted to do so, he was set on shore at Douglas. It happened to be a fine moon-light night, and very dry, being a small frost; he therefore forebore going into any house to refresh himself, but made the best of his way to the house of a sister he had at Kirk Merlugh. As he was going over a pretty high mountain, he heard the noise of horses, the hollow of a huntsman, and the finest horn in the world. He was a little surprised that anybody pursued those kinds of sports in the night, but he had not time for much reflection before they all passed by him, so near that he was able to count what number there was of

Above: *The Fairy Queen – A Procession*, Charles Doyle (1832–93)

them, which he said was thirteen, and that they were all drest in green, and gallantly mounted. He was so well pleased with the sight, that he would gladly have followed, could he have kept pace with them; he crossed the footway, however, that he might see them again, which he did more than once, and lost not the sound of the horn for some miles. At length, being arrived at his sister's, he tells her the story, who presently clapped her hands for joy, that he was come home safe; for, said she, those you saw were fairies, and 'tis well they did not take you away with them. There is no persuading them but that these huntings are frequent in the island, and that these little gentry being too proud to ride on Manx horses, which they might find in a field, make use of the English and Irish ones, which are brought over and kept by gentlemen. They say nothing is more common, than to find these poor beasts in a morning, all over in a sweat and foam, and tired almost to death.

George Waldron, *The History and Description of the Isle of Man*, 1744

THE AIRBORNE RADE

The thunder's noise is our delight,
And lightning makes us day by night,
And in the air we dance on high
To the loud music of the sky.

About the moon we make a ring,
And falling stars we wanton fling
Like squibs and rockets, for a toy,
While what frights others is our joy.

But when we'd hunt away our cares
We boldly mount the galloping spheres;
And riding so from east to west,
We chase each nimble zodiac beast.

Thus, giddy grown, we make our beds,
With thick black clouds to rest our heads,
And flood the earth with our dark showers,
That did but sprinkle these our bowers.

Thus having done with orbs and sky,
Those mightly spaces vast and high,
Then down we come, and take the shapes
Sometimes of cats, sometimes of apes.

Anonymous English poem, seventeenth century

Opposite: *Fairies*, Anonymous, nineteenth century

A FÆRIE CAULDRON

IN THE VESTRY HERE, on the North side of the chancel, is an extraordinary great kettle or cauldron, which the inhabitants say, by tradition, was brought hither by the fairies, time out of mind, from Borough hill, about a mile from hence. To this place, if anyone went to borrow a yoke of oxen, money etc., he might have it for a year or longer, so he

The Pixie's Meal, Rosa C. Petherick

kept his word to return it. There is a cave, where some have fancied to hear music. On this Borough hill (in the tything of Cherte, in the parish of Frensham) is a great stone lying along, of the length of about six feet: they went to this stone, and knocked at it, and declared what they would borrow, and when they would repay, and a voice would answer, when they should come, and that they should find what they desired to borrow at that stone. This cauldron, with the trivet, was borrowed here after the manner aforesaid, but not returned according to promise; and though the cauldron was afterwards carried to the stone, it could not be received, and ever since that time no borrowing there. The people saw a great fire one night (not long since), the next day they went to see if any heath was burnt there, but found nothing . . . These stories are verily believed by most of the old women of this parish, and by many of their daughters . . . I remember the very same tradition and belief is in and about Camelot in Somersetshire, where King Arthur kept his court.

John Aubrey, *The Natural History and Antiquities of the County of Surrey*, 1684

OBERON'S FEAST

And now we must imagine, first,
The elves present, to quench his thirst,
A pure seed-pearl of infant dew
Brought and besweetened in a blue
And pregnant violet; which done,
His kitling eyes begin to run
Quite through the table, where he spies
The horns of papery butterflies:
Of which he eats, and tastes a little

Above: Detail of *The Fairies' Banquet*, John Anster Fitzgerald

Of that we call the cuckoo's spittle.
A little fuzz-ball pudding stands
By, yet not blessed by his hands;
That was too coarse: but then forthwith
He ventures boldly on the pith
Of sugared rush, and eats the sagg
And well-bestrutted bee's sweet bag:
Gladding his palate with some store
Of emmets' eggs: what would he more?
But beards of mice, a newt's stewed thigh,
A bloated earwig and a fly;
With the red-capped worm that's shut
Within the concave of a nut,
Brown as his tooth. A little moth
Late fattened in a piece of cloth:
With withered cherries, mandrakes' ears,
Moles' eyes; to these the slain stag's tears,
The unctuous dewlaps of a snail,
The broke-heart of a nightingale
O'ercome in music; with a wine . . .
Brought in a dainty daisy, which
He fully quaffs up to bewitch
His blood to height; this done, commended
Grace by his priest; the feast is ended.

Robert Herrick, 1591–1674

A FÆRIE FAIR

 N THE SIDE OF A HILL, named Blackdown, between the parishes of Pittminster, and Chestonford, not many miles from Taunton, those that have had occasion to travel that way, have frequently seen them there, appearing like men and women of a stature, generally, near the smaller size of men; their habits used to be of red, blue, or green, according to the old way of country garb, with high crowned hats. One time about 50 years since, a person (living at Combe St Nicholas, a parish lying on one side of that hill, near Chard) was

Above: *Goblin Harvest*, Amelia M. Bowerley (d. 1919)

riding towards his home that way; and saw just before him, on the side of the hill a great company of people, that seemed to him like country folks, assembled, as at a fair; there was all sorts of commodities to his appearance, as at our ordinary fairs; pewterers, shoemakers, pedlars, with all kinds of trinkets, fruit, and drinking booths; he could not remember any thing which he had usually seen at fairs, but what he saw there . . . he was under very great surprise, and admired what the meaning of what he saw should be; at length it came into his mind what he had heard concerning the fairies on

Above: *The Enchanted Forest*, John Anster Fitzgerald

the side of that hill: and it being near the road he was to take,
he resolved to ride in amongst them, and see what they were;
accordingly he put on his horse that way; and thought he saw them
perfectly all along as he came, yet when he was upon the place where
all this had appeared to him, he could discern nothing at all, only
seemed to be crowded, and thrust, as when one passes through a
throng of people: all the rest became invisible to him, until he came
at a little distance, and then it appeared to him again as at first.
He found himself in pain, and so hasted home; whence being
arrived, a lameness seized him all on one side, which continued on
him as long as he lived . . .

Richard Bovet, *Pandaemonium*, 1684

THE FÆRIE KNIGHT, PIGWIGGEN

And quickly arms him for the field,
A little cockleshell his shield,
Which he could very bravely wield:
Yet could it not be pierced:
His spear a bent both stiff and strong,
And well near of two inches long;
The pyle was of a horsefly's tongue,
Whose sharpness nought reversed.

And puts him on a coat of mail,
Which was of a fish's scale,
That when his foe should him assail,
No point should be prevailing:
His rapier was a hornet's sting,
It was a very dangerous thing:
For if he chanced to hurt the King,
It would be long in healing.

Above: *The Midsummer Fairies*, John George Nash (1824–1905)

His helmet was a beetle's head,
Most horrible and full of dread,
That able was to strike one dead,
Yet did it well become him:
And for a plume, a horse's hair,
Which being tossed with the air,
Had force to strike his foe with fear,
And turn his weapon from him.

Himself, he on a earwig set,
Yet scarce he on his back could get,
So oft and high he did curvet,
Ere he himself could settle:
He made him turn and stop, and bound,
To gallop, and to trot the round,
He scarce could stand on any ground,
He was so full of mettle.

Michael Drayton, 1563–1631, *Nimphidia*

CHAPTER THREE

FÆRIE FOLK

HE MOST FAMOUS INDIVIDUAL FAIRY IS PUCK, also called Robin Goodfellow, known from Shakespeare's play, *A Midsummer Night's Dream*. But in færie lore Puck is a type, not just an individual, whose other names include Pug, Pookha, Will o' the Wisp, Jack o' Lantern and Friar Rush. These lead travellers into bogs with flickering lights, throw furniture around inside the house, or ride the horses all night, leaving them exhausted and sweating in the stable by morning, their manes tangled into elf-locks or fairy stirrups.

Some solitary færies are tied to a place. Brownies usually belong to a house, where they help with domestic chores in return for a bowl of milk or food. Occasionally they belong to a family, and move house with them. They will disappear if they are given a new suit of clothes. The poet John Milton called his household fairy a goblin or 'the lubber feind', a name now more familiar to us as Lob-lie-by-the-fire.

Other solitary færies are attached to outdoor sites, like the North Country Brown Man of the Muirs, or the Yorkshire Church Grim who lives in churches and tolls the bells at midnight. In Ireland leprechauns are often found in a hillock or near a hawthorn bush. They are cobblers

Opposite: Detail of *The Marriage of Oberon and Titania*, John Anster Fitzgerald

Friar Puck, Henry Fuseli (1741–1825)

and tinkers, and can be heard hammering away. Sometimes they can be tricked into telling human beings the whereabouts of their hoard of gold.

Other færies live in lakes, rivers and the sea. There are nixies or gwragedd annwn, Welsh water maidens, living in lakes, who will marry humans, and mermen and mermaids, in the sea. In Scottish lochs live the more dangerous kelpies, which take the form of horses or handsome young men who lure humans into the water.

'Elf' is the Anglo-Saxon name for færies in general and in Scottish poems 'elfame' is the word for færie land, the dwelling of the færie court. Today we tend to think of færies as females and elves as males, but in older times elves was just a general term for any færie. 'Dwarf' is a term used to describe any small færie.

Other terms include imps, boggarts, goblins, hobgoblins and hobs. Imps are definitely small devils, boggarts are brownies, and goblins (the same as hobgoblins and hobs) may be related to the sometimes friendly knockers or coblynau heard working in the mines. Goblins often frighten humans, but their more glamorous cousins may be just as dangerous.

SHAKESPEARE'S PUCK

FAIRY: Either I mistake your shape and making quite,
Or else you are that shrewd and knavish sprite,
Called Robin Goodfellow; are you not he,
That fright the maidens of the villagery;
Skim milk; and sometimes labour in the quern;
And bootless make the breathless housewife churn;
And sometime make the drink to bear no barm;
Mislead night-wanderers, laughing at their harm?
Those that Hobgoblin call you, and sweet Puck,
You do their work, and they shall have good luck.
Are not you he?

PUCK: Thou speak'st aright;
I am that merry wanderer of the night.
I jest to Oberon, and make him smile,
When I a fat bean-fed horse beguile,
Neighing in the likeness of a silly foal:
And sometime lurk I in a gossip's bowl,
In the very likeness of a roasted crab;
And, when she drinks, against her lips I bob,
And on her withered dewlap pour the ale.
The wisest aunt, telling the saddest tale,
Sometime for three-foot stool mistaketh me;

Then slip I from her bum, down topples she,
And 'tailor' cries and falls into a cough . . .

William Shakespeare, *A Midsummer Night's Dream*, 1596

Above: *Puck*, Sir Joshua Reynolds (1723–92)

THE BROWN MAN OF THE MOORS

N THE YEAR BEFORE THE great Rebellion, two young men from Newcastle were sporting on the High Moors above Elsdon . . . The younger lad ran to the brook for water; and, after stooping to drink, was surprised, on lifting his head again, by the appearance of a brown dwarf, who stood on a crag covered with brackens across the burn. This extraordinary personage did not appear to be above half the stature of a common man; but was uncommonly stout and

Above: *Jack O' Lantern*, Arthur Hughes (1832–1915)

broad-built, having the appearance of vast strength; his dress was entirely brown, the colour of the brackens, and his head covered with frizzled red hair; his countenance was expressive of the most savage ferocity, and his eyes glared like a bull.

It seems he addressed the young man: first threatening him with his vengeance for having trespassed on his demesnes, and asking him if he knew in whose presence he stood? The youth replied that he supposed him to be the Lord of the Moors; that he had offended through ignorance, and offered to bring him the game he had killed. The dwarf . . . remarked that nothing could be more offensive to him than such an offer; as he considered the wild animals as his subjects, and never failed to avenge their destruction. He condescended further to inform him, that he was, like himself, mortal, though of years far exceeding the lot of common humanity, and (what I should not have had an idea of) that he hoped for salvation . . . Finally he invited his new acquaintance to accompany him home, and partake his hospitality; an offer which the youth was on the point of accepting, and was just going to spring across the brook (which if he had done . . . the dwarf would certainly have torn him in pieces,) when his foot was arrested by the voice of his companion, who thought he tarried long, and on looking round again, 'the wee Brown Man was fled'. The story adds, that he was imprudent enough to slight the admonition, and to sport over the Moors on his way homewards; but soon after his return, he fell into a lingering disorder, and died within the year.

Robert Surtees, in a letter to Walter Scott, *c.* 1809

THE LUBBER FIEND

Sometimes, with secure delight
The upland hamlets will invite
When the merry bells ring round
And the jocund rebecks sound

Above: *Contradiction Oberon and Titania*, Richard Dadd

To many a youth and many a maid
Dancing in the chequered shade,
And young and old come forth to play
On a sunshine holyday,
Till the livelong daylight fail:
Then to the spicey nut-brown ale,
With stories told of many a feat:
How fairy Mab the junket eat;
She was pinched and pulled, she said;
And he, by friar's lantern led,
Tells how the drudging goblin sweat
To earn his cream-bowl duly set,
When, in one night, ere glimpse of morn,
His shadowy flail hath threshed the corn
That ten day-labourers could not end;
Then lies him down the lubber fiend,
And, stretched out all the chimney's length,
Basks at the fire his hairy strength,
And crop-full, out of doors he flings,
Ere the first cock his matin rings.
Thus done the tales, to bed they creep,
By whispering winds soon lulled asleep.

John Milton, 'L'Allegro', c. 1632–37

Opposite: *The Time I've Lost in Wooing*, Daniel MacLise (1806–70)

BROWNIES

ROWNIE IS A PERSONAGE OF small stature, wrinkled visage, covered with short curly brown hair, and wearing a brown mantle and hood. His residence is in the hollow of an old tree, a ruined castle, or the abode of man. He is attached to particular families, with whom he has been known to reside, even for centuries, threshing the corn, cleaning the house, and doing everything done by his northern and English brethren. He is, to a certain degree, disinterested; like many great personages, he is shocked at anything approaching to the name of a bribe or douceur, yet, like them, allows his scruples to be overcome if the thing be done in a genteel, delicate, and secret way. Thus, offer Brownie a piece of bread, a cup of drink, or a new coat and hood, and he flouted at it, and perhaps, in his huff quitted the place for ever; but leave a nice bowl of cream, and some fresh honeycomb, in a snug private corner, and they soon disappeared, though Brownie, it was to be supposed, never knew anything of them.

A good woman had just made a web of lindsey-woolsey, and, prompted by her good-nature, had manufactured from it a snug mantle and hood for her little Brownie. Not content with laying the gift in one of his favourite spots, she indiscreetly called to tell him it was there. This was too direct, and Brownie quitted the place, crying,

'A new mantle and a new hood!
'Poor Brownie! ye'll ne'er do mair gude!'

Thomas Keightley, *The Fairy Mythology*, 1850

THE LEPRECHAUN

Lay your ear close to the hill,
  Do you not catch the tiny clamour,
  Busy click of an elfin hammer,
Voice of the Leprechaun singing shrill,
  As he busily plies his trade? . . .

Above: Detail of *Fairies in a Bird's Nest*, John Anster Fitzgerald

I caught him at work one day, myself,
In the castle-ditch, where foxglove grows;
A wrinkled, wizened, and bearded Elf,
    Spectacles stuck on his pointed nose,
    Silver buckles to his hose,
Leather apron – shoe in his lap –
    'Tip-rap, tip-tap,
    Tick-tack-too,
    (A grasshopper on my cap!
        Away the moth flew!)
    Buskins for a fairy prince,
        Brogues for his son –
    Pay me well, pay me well
        When the job is done!'
The rogue was mine, beyond a doubt.
    I stared at him; he stared at me;
    'Servant, Sir!' 'Humph!' says he,
And pulled a snuffbox out.
He took a long pinch, looked better pleased,
    The queer little Leprechaun;
Offered the box with a whimsical grace –
Pouf! he flung the dust in my face,
    And while I sneezed,
        Was gone!

William Allingham, 1824–89

MINERS AND KNOCKERS

NDER THE GENERAL TITLE of Coblynau I class the fairies which haunt the mines, quarries and underground regions of Wales, corresponding to the cabalistic gnomes. The word coblyn has the double meaning of knocker or thumper and sprite or fiend; and may it not be the original of goblin? It is applied by Welsh miners to pigmy fairies which dwell in the mines, and point out, by a peculiar knocking or rapping, rich veins of ore. The faith is extended, in some parts, so as to cover the indication of subterranean treasures generally, in caves and secret places of the mountains. The coblynau are described as being about half a yard in height and very ugly to look upon, but extremely good-natured, and warm friends of the miner. Their dress is a grotesque imitation of the miner's garb, and they carry tiny hammers, picks and lamps. They work busily, loading ore in buckets, flitting about the shafts, turning tiny windlasses, and pounding away like madmen, but really accomplishing nothing whatever. They have been known to throw stones at the miners, when enraged by being lightly spoken of; but the stones are harmless. Nevertheless, all miners of a proper spirit refrain from provoking them, because their presence brings good luck.

Wirt Sikes, *British Goblins*, 1880

[65]

A LAKE FÆRIE

ELSHMAN TELL US OF another thing, not a miracle but a marvel. They say that Gwestin of Gwestiniog waited and watched near Brecknock Mere (Langorse Lake), which is some two miles around, and saw, on three brilliant moonlight nights, bands of dancing women in his fields of oats, and that he followed these until they sank in the water of the pond; and that, on the fourth night, he detained one of the maidens. The ravisher's version of the incident was that on each of the nights after they had sunk, he had heard them murmuring under the water and saying, 'Had he done thus and so, he would have caught one of us'; and he said that he had thus been taught by their lips how to capture this maiden, who yielded and married him. Her first words to her husband were: 'I shall willingly serve thee with full obedience and devotion until that day when in your eagerness to hasten to the shouting (*clamores*) beyond Llyfni you will strike me with your bridle-rein.' Now Llyfni is a river near the pond. And this thing came to pass. After the birth of many children, she was struck by him with his bridle-rein and, on his return from his ride, he found her fleeing with all her offspring. Pursuing, he snatched away with great difficulty one of his sons, Triunein Nagelauc (Trinio Faglog) by name . . .

Walter Map, *c.* 1140–1210, *De Nugis Curialium*

Above: *Oberon and the Mermaid*, Sir Joseph Noel Paton

CHAPTER FOUR

FÆRIE ENCOUNTERS

ENCOUNTERS WITH FÆRIES MUST BE TREATED with the greatest caution. True, the occasional good brownie will work for years without pay, but all færies, even brownies, are unpredictable creatures, quick to take offence. 'Anno 1670, not far from Cirencester, was an apparition,' wrote the antiquary John Aubrey: 'being demanded, whether a good spirit, or a bad? returned no answer, but disappeared with a curious perfume and most melodious twang. Mr. W. Lilly believes it was a fairy.'

People who have stumbled on færies dancing have often lived to regret it. Some have woken from what seemed like an evening's dancing to discover that years have passed, for færie time is not our time. Those who have eaten food or drink offered them have found that they are in thrall to the færie court and cannot return to the ordinary world. For færies often capture human beings, sometimes leaving in their place an enchanted look-alike made out of an old log. Musicians may be lured away to play for fairies; young men may be enticed to their doom by water færies. Beautiful young girls are kidnapped by færies to become their lovers or sometimes merely servants.

Middle-aged wives and mothers risk being kidnapped to be

Opposite: Detail of *Watching the Fairies*, Beatrice Goldsmith (1895–1947)

midwives to a færie birth or nurses to the baby, for færie births are difficult and færie babies often do not thrive. (If lucky, the midwives or nurses will be allowed to return, after their task is completed.) Unbaptized human babies are also stolen, and in their place are left changelings. These are often wizened or sickly, which is perhaps why færies prefer human children or need to capture human wet nurses. Occasionally færies can be tricked into restoring the original child.

But usually only the bold have a chance of rescuing somebody from the færies. It takes great courage to lie in wait for a færie rade to pass by, or to go to the færie mound, armed only with cold iron, a metal which was sometimes an effective shield against enchantment. Robert Kirk, the great færie historian, was captured by the færies at the age of forty-two in 1688, so it is said. Though his gravestone is in Aberfoyle church, where his body was apparently buried, he is to this day still imprisoned in the færie mound.

INTERRUPTING THE DANCE

N THE YEAR 1633–4, soon after I had entered into my grammar at the Latin School at Yatton Keynel (near Chippenham, Wilts), our curate, Mr Hart, was annoyed one night by these elves or fairies. Coming over the downs, it being near dark, and approaching one of the fairy

Above: *The Dance of the Little People*, William Holmes Sullivan (d. 1908)

dances, as the common people call them in these parts, viz. the green circles made by those sprites on the grass, he all at once saw an innumerable quantity of pigmies or very small people, dancing

Above: The Fairy Queen, Sir Joseph Noel Paton

round and round, and singing, and making all manner of small odd noises. He, being very greatly amazed, and yet not being able, as he says, to run away from them, being, as he supposes, kept there in a kind of enchantment, they no sooner perceive him but they surround him on all sides, and what betwixt fear and amazement, he fell down scarcely knowing what he did; and thereupon these little creatures pinched him all over, and made a sort of quick humming noise all the time; but at length they left him, and when the sun rose, he found himself exactly in the midst of one of these fairy dances. This relation I had from him myself, a few days after he was so tormented; but when I and my bedfellow Stump went soon afterwards, at night time to the dances on the downs, we saw none of the elves or fairies. But, indeed, it is said they seldom appear to any persons who go to seek for them.

Attributed to John Aubrey, 1626–97

THOMAS THE RHYMER

True Thomas lay on Huntlier bank;
A ferlie he spied wi' his e'e;
And there he saw a lady bright,
Come riding down by the Eildon Tree.

Her skirt was o' the grass green silk,
Her mantle o' the velvet fine,
At ilka tett of her horse's mane
Hang fifty siller bells and nine.

True Thomas he pulled aff his cap
And louted low down to his knee:
'All hail, thou mighty Queen of Heaven!
For thy peer on earth I never did see.'

'O no, O no, Thomas,' she said,
'That name does not belang to me;
I am but the queen of fair Elfland,
That am hither come to visit thee.

Harp and carp, Thomas,' she said,
'Harp and carp, along wi' me,
And if he dare to kiss my lips,
Sure of your bodie I will be!'

'Betide me weal, betide me woe,
That weird sall never daunton me';
Syne he has kissed her rosy lips,
All underneath the Eildon Tree.

Opposite: *Titania*, John Simmons

'Now, ye maun go wi' me,' she said,
'True Thomas, ye maun go wi' me,
And ye maun serve me seven years,
Thro' weal or woe as may chance to be . . .'

'But, Thomas, ye maun hold your tongue,
Whatever ye may hear or see,
For, if you speak word in Elflyn land,
Ye'll ne'er get back to your ain countrie' . . .

Syne they came on to a garden green,
And she pu'd an apple fræ the tree:
'Take this for thy wages, True Thomas,
It will give the tongue that can never lie.'

'My tongue is mine ain,' True Thomas said,
'A gudely gift ye wad gie to me!
I neither dought to buy nor sell,
At fair or tryst where I may be . . .'

He has gotten a coat of the even cloth,
And a pair of shoes of velvet green,
And till seven years were gane and past
True Thomas on earth was never seen.

Traditional Scottish ballad

Above: *The Haunt of the Fairies*, Richard Dadd

A FÆRIE BARGAIN

ANOTHER INSTANCE . . . was told me by a person who had the reputation of the utmost integrity. This man being desirous of disposing of a horse he had at that time no great occasion for, and riding him to market for that purpose, was accosted, in passing over the mountains, by a little man in a plain dress, who asked him if he would sell his horse.

'Tis the design I am going on, replied the person who told me the story. On which, the other desired to know the price. Eight pounds, said he. No, resumed the purchaser, I will give no more than seven; which, if you will take, here is your money. The owner thinking he had bid pretty fair, agreed with him, and the money being told out, the one dismounted, and the other got on the back of the horse, which he had no sooner done, than both beast and rider sunk into the earth immediately, leaving the person who had made the bargain in the utmost terror and consternation. As soon as he had a little recovered himself, he went directly to the parson of the parish, and related what had passed, desiring he would give his opinion whether he ought to make use of the money he had received or not. To which he replied, that as he had made a fair bargain, and no way circumvented, nor endeavoured to circumvent the buyer, he saw no reason to believe, in case it was an evil spirit, it could have any power over him. On this assurance, he went home well satisfied, and nothing afterward happened to give him any disquiet concerning this affair.

George Waldron, *The History and Description of the Isle of Man*, 1744

Opposite: *The Enchanted Forest*, Sir John Gilbert (1817–97)

A FÆRIE CAPTURED

MAN WHO LIVED AT the foot of Trendreen hill, in the valley of Treridge, I think, was cutting furze on the hill. Near the middle of the day he saw one of the small people, not more than a foot long, stretched at full length and fast asleep, on a bank of griglans [heath], surrounded by high brakes of furze. The man took off his furze cuff [glove], and slipped the little man into it, without his waking up; went down to the house, took the little fellow out of the cuff on the hearthstone, when he awaked and seemed quite pleased and at home, beginning to play with the children, who were well pleased with the small body, and called him Bobby Griglans.

The old people were very careful not to let Bob out of the house, or be seen by the neighbours, as he promised to show the man where the crocks of gold were buried on the hill. A few days after he was brought from the hill, all the neighbours came with their horses (according to custom) to bring home the winter's reek of furze, which had to be brought down the hill in trusses on the backs of the horses. That Bob might be safe and out of sight, he and the children were shut up in the barn. Whilst the furze-carriers were in to dinner, the prisoners contrived to get out, to have a 'courant' round the furze-reek, when they saw a little man and woman, not much larger

Opposite: *Hermia and Lysander*, John Simmons

than Bob, searching into every hole and corner among the trusses that were dropped round the unfinished reek. The little woman was wringing her hands and crying, 'O my dear and tender Skillywidden, wherever canst ah [thou] be gone to? shall I ever cast eyes on thee again?' 'Go'e back,' says Bob to the children; 'my father and mother are come here too.' He then cried out, 'Here I am, mammy!' By the time the words were out of his mouth, the little man and woman with their precious Skillywidden, were nowhere to be seen . . .

Robert Hunt, *Popular Romances of the West of England*, 1881

THE CHANGELING

 YOUNG WOMAN, whose name was Mary Scannell, lived with her husband not many years ago at Castle Martyr. One day in harvest time she went with several more to help in binding up the wheat, and left the child, which she was nursing, in a corner of the field, quite safe, as she thought, wrapped up in her cloak. When her work was finished, she returned to where the child was, but in place of her own, she found a thing in the cloak that was not half the size, and that kept up such a crying you might have heard it a mile off. So Mary Scannell guessed how the case stood, and without stop or stay, away she took it in her arms, pretending to be mighty fond of it all the while, to a wise woman. The wise woman told her in a whisper not to give it enough to eat, and to beat and pinch it without mercy, which Mary Scannell did; and just in one week after to the day, when she awoke in the morning, she found her own child lying by her side in the bed! The fairy that had been put in its place did not like the usage it got from Mary Scannell, who understood how to treat it, like a sensible woman as she was, and away it went, after a week's trial and sent her own child back to her.

T. Crofton Croker, *Fairy Legends and Traditions of the South of Ireland*, 1826

Opposite: *Rabbit among the Fairies*, John Anster Fitzgerald

SONG OF THE FÆRIE FOSTER-MOTHER

Bright Eyes, Light Eyes! Daughter of a Fay!
I had not been a married wife a twelvemonth and a day,
I had not nurst my little one a month upon my knee,
When down among the bluebell banks rose elfins three times three,
They gript me by the raven hair, I could not cry for fear,
They put a hempen rope around my waist and dragged me here,
They made me sit and give thee suck as mortal mothers can,
Bright Eyes, Light Eyes! strange and weak and wan!

Dim Face, Grim Face! lie ye there so still?
Thy red red lips are at my breast, and thou may'st suck thy fill;
But know ye, tho' I hold thee firm, and rock thee to and fro,
'Tis not to soothe thee into sleep, but just to still my woe?
And know ye, when I lean so calm against the wall of stone,
'Tis when I shut my eyes and try to think thou art
mine own?
And know ye, tho' my milk be here, my heart
is far away,
Dim Face, Grim Face! Daughter of a Fay!

Weak Thing, Meek Thing! take
   no blame from me,
Altho' my babe may fade for
   lack of what I give to thee;
For though thou art a stranger
   thing, and though thou art
   my woe,
To feed thee sucking at my
   breast is all the joy I know,
It soothes me tho' afar away I
   hear my daughter call,
My heart were broken if I felt
   no little lips at all!
If I had none to tend at all, to
   be its nurse and slave,
Weak Thing, Meek Thing!
   I should shriek and rave!

Robert Buchanan, 1841–91

Above: *Once upon a Time*, Henry Maynell Rheam

A STOLEN WIFE

AMONG OTHER INSTANCES of undoubted verity, proving in these the being of such aereal people, or species of creatures not vulgarly known, I add the subsequent relations, some whereof I have from my acquaintance with the actors and patients, and the rest from the eye witnesses to the matter of fact. The first whereof shall be of the woman taken out of her childbed, and having a lingering image of her substituted body in her room, which resemblance decayed, died and was buried. But the person stolen returning to her husband after two years space, he being convinced by many undeniable tokens that she was his former wife, admitted her home, and had diverse children by her. Among other reports she gave her husband, this was one: that she perceived little what they did in the spacious house she lodged in, until she anointed one of her eyes with a certain unction, that was by her; which they perceiving to have acquainted her with their actions, they fained her blind of that eye with a puff of their breath. She found the place full of light, without any fountain or lamp from whence it did spring. This person lived in the country next to that of my last residence . . .

Robert Kirk, *The Secret Commonwealth*, 1691

Opposite: *The Lover's World*, Eleanor Fortescue–Brickdale (1871–1945)

[86]

THE LAST SIGHT OF
ROBERT KIRK

THE REVEREND ROBERT KIRK ... was walking, it is said, one evening in his night-gown, upon the little eminence to the west of the present manse, which is still reckoned a *Dun shi'* (a fairy mound). He fell down dead, as was believed; but this was not his fate ... Mr Kirk

Above: *Titania*, Frederick Howard Michael (d. 1936)

was the near relation of Graham of Duchray . . . Shortly after his funeral, he appeared in the dress in which he had sunk down, to a mutual relation of his own and of Duchray. 'Go,' said he to him, 'to my cousin Duchray, and tell him that I am not dead; I fell down in a swoon, and was carried into Fairy-land, where I now am. Tell him, that when he and my friends are assembled at the baptism of my child (for he had left his wife pregnant) I will appear in the room, and that if he throws the knife which he holds in his hand over my head, I will be released, and restored to human society.' The man, it seems, neglected, for some time, to deliver the message. Mr Kirk appeared to him a second time, threatening to haunt him night and day till he executed his commission, which, at length, he did. The time of the baptism arrived. They were seated at table; Mr Kirk entered, but the laird of Duchray, by some unaccountable fatality, neglected to perform the prescribed ceremony. Mr Kirk retired by another door, and was seen no more. It is firmly believed that he is, at this day, in Fairy-land.

Revd Patrick Graham, *Sketches of Perthshire*, 1812

CHAPTER FIVE

FAREWELL TO FÆRIES

LTHOUGH TIME PASSES FOR FÆRIES IN A different way than for us, and their life spans are much longer, færies are mortal beings too. Human onlookers have stumbled across their funerals, occasions of great grief. Death to them is more terrible than it is to us. They have no hope of life after death, no hope of heaven, because they have no souls.

A færie king once asked an Irish saint if there could be any chance of being restored to heaven among the angels. The last judgement day, said the saint, would bring about their total annihilation. This doom hangs over the færies, as they dance and sing here on earth. 'Some say their continual sadness is because of their pendulous state . . . as uncertain what at the last Revolution will become of them . . . ; and if they have any frolic fits of mirth, 'tis as the constrained grinning of a mort-head,' reported the Reverend Kirk.

Most people believe that færies are dying out or have already become extinct. In fact, prophets of doom have been lamenting their disappearance for the last six hundred years. As long ago as the fourteenth century, the English poet Geoffrey Chaucer claimed that færies had disappeared from the countryside. He blamed the new Catholic

Opposite: Detail of *The Fairy Queen*, Richard Painton (fl. *c.* 1900)

friars for driving the good folk away. Three centuries later, a different reason was being given for their disappearance. The Bishop of Norwich, Richard Corbet, decided that færies had been Catholics. He thought that the Reformation and the advent of the Puritans had seen them off.

Today the death of the færies continues to be discussed. My father used to show me an Army camp outside Taunton, opposite a filling station. 'My cousin used to tell me that this is where the last færie in Somerset appeared,' he said. He knew nothing more than this: no last words, no details of the farewell, just this single melancholy fact.

So each human generation mourns the ending of the færie kingdom and each human generation tells the stories of how færies used to be more common. This curious paradox, in which the færie race is always vanishing yet has never vanished, continues down the centuries. Perhaps the truth is that the unseen world never wholly vanishes.

Opposite: *Titania*, John Simmons

THE VANISHING FÆRIES

Deep in the wood's recesses cool
I see the fairy dancers glide,
In cloth of gold, in gown of green,
My lord and lady side by side.

But who has hung from leaf to leaf,
From flower to flower, a silken twine —
A cloud of grey that holds the dew
In globes of clean enchanted wine?

Or stretches far from branch to branch,
From thorn to thorn, in diamond rain,
Who caught the cup of crystal pure
And hung so fair the shining chain?

'Tis death, the spider, in his net,
Who lures the dancers as they glide,
In cloth of gold, in gown of green,
My lord and lady, side by side.

Dora Sigerson Shorter, 1866–1918

Opposite: *The Fairy's Funeral*, John Anster Fitzgerald

A FÆRIE FUNERAL SEEN BY THE POET WILLIAM BLAKE

LAKE'S MIND . . . could convert the most ordinary occurrence into something mystical and supernatural. He often saw less majestic shapes than those of the poets of old. 'Did you ever see a fairy's funeral, madam?' he once said to a lady, who happened to sit by him in company. 'Never, sir!' was the answer. 'I have,' said Blake, 'but not before last night. I was walking alone in my garden, there was great stillness among the branches and flowers and more than common sweetness in the air; I heard a low and pleasant sound, and I knew not whence it came. At last I saw the broad leaf of a flower move, and underneath I saw a procession of creatures of the size and colour of green and grey grasshoppers, bearing a body laid out on a rose leaf, which they buried with songs, and then disappeared. It was a fairy funeral.' It would have perhaps been better for his fame had he connected it more with the superstitious beliefs of his country — amongst the elves and fairies his fancy might have wandered at will — their popular character would perhaps have kept him within the bounds of traditionary belief, and the sea of his imagination might have had a shore.

Allan Cunningham, *The British Painters*, 1833

Opposite: Detail of *The Fairy Wood*, Henry Maynell Rheam

HOW FRIARS HAVE DRIVEN AWAY FÆRIES

In th' old days of the king Arthur,
Of which that Britons speken great honour,
All was this land fulfilled of faierye.
The elf-queen, with her jolly company,
Danced full oft in many a green mead;
This was the old opinion, as I rede.
I speak of many hundred years ago;
But now no man can see none elves mo.
For now the great charity and prayers
Of limitours and other holy friars,
That serchen every land and every stream,
As thick as motes in the sonne-beam,
Blessing halles, chambers, kitchens, bowers,
Cities, burghes, castles, high towers,
Thropes, barnes, shipnes, dairies,
This maketh that there been no fairies.
For there as wont to walkne was an elf,
Therer walketh now the limitour himself . . .

Geoffrey Chaucer, *Canterbury Tales*, c. 1387

HOW PROTESTANTS HAVE DRIVEN AWAY FÆRIES

Farewell, rewards and fairies,
Good housewives now may say,
For now foul sluts in dairies
Do fare as well as they;
And though they sweep their hearth no less
Than maids were wont to do,
Yet who of late for cleanliness,
Finds sixpence in her shoe.

Lament, lament old abbeys,
The fairies lost command,
They did but change priests' babies,
But some have changed your hand;
And all your children stol'n from thence
Are now grown puritans,
Who live as changelings ever since
For love of your demesnes . . .

Witness those rings and roundelays
Of theirs which yet remain,
Were footed in Queen Mary's days

On many a grassy plain.
But since of late Elizabeth
And later James came in,
They never danced on any heath
As when the time had been.

By which we note the fairies
Were of the old profession,
Their songs were *Ave Maries*,
Their dances were procession;
But now alas, they all are dead
Or gone beyond the seas,
Or further from religion fled,
Or else they take their ease . . .

Richard Corbet, Bishop of Norwich, 1582–1634

Opposite: Detail of *What the Little Girl Saw in the Bush*, Frederick McCubbin (1855–1917)

HOW FACTORIES HAVE DRIVEN AWAY FÆRIES

THE OTHER DAY I passed up the Hollow, which tradition says was once green, and lone, and wild; and there I saw the manufacturer's day dreams embodied in substantial stone and brick and ashes — the cinder-black highway, the cottages, and the cottage gardens; there I saw a mighty mill, and a chimney, ambitious as the Tower of Babel. I told my old housekeeper when I came home where I had been.

'Ay,' said she; 'this world has queer changes. I can remember the old mill being built — the very first it was in all the district; and then I can remember it being pulled down and going with my lake-lasses [companions] to see the foundation-stone of the new one laid . . .'

'What was the Hollow like then, Martha?'

'Different to what it is now; but I can tell of it clean different again, when there was neither mill, nor cot, nor hall, except Fieldhead, within two miles of it. I can tell, one summer evening, fifty years syne, my mother coming running in just at the edge of dark, almost fleyed out of her wits, saying she had seen a fairish [fairy] in Fieldhead Hollow and that was the last fairish that was ever seen on this countryside (though they've been heard within these forty years).'

Charlotte Brontë, *Shirley*, 1849

THE PARTING OF THE FÆRIES

N A SABBATH MORNING, nearly sixty years ago, all the inmates of this little hamlet (near Glend Eathie) had gone to church, except a herdboy, and a little girl, his sister, who were lounging beside one of the cottages, when just as the shadow of the garden-dial had fallen on the line of noon, they saw a long cavalcade ascending out of the ravine, through the wooded hollow. It winded among the knolls and bushes; and, turning round the northern gable of the cottage, beside which the sole spectators of the scene were stationed, began to ascend the eminence towards the south. The horses were shaggy diminutive things, speckled dun and grey; the riders stunted, misgrown, ugly creatures, attired in antique jerkins of plaid, long grey cloaks, and little red caps, from under which their wild uncombed locks shot out over their cheeks and foreheads. The boy and his sister stood gazing in utter dismay and astonishment, as rider after rider, each more uncouth and dwarfish than the other which had preceded it, passed the cottage and disappeared among the brushwood, which at that period covered the hill, until at length the entire rout, except the last rider, who lingered a few yards behind the others, had gone by.

'What are ye, little mannie? and where are ye going?' inquired the boy, his curiosity getting the better of his fears and prudence.

'Not of the race of Adam,' said the creature, turning for a

moment in its saddle: 'The People of Peace shall never more be seen in Scotland.'

Hugh Miller, *Old Red Sandstone*, 1887

THE HORNS OF ELFLAND

The splendour falls on castle walls
    And snowy summits old in story:
The long light shakes across the lakes
    And the wild cataract leaps in glory,
Blow, bugle, blow, set the wild echoes flying,
Blow, bugle; answer, echoes, dying, dying, dying.

O hark, O hear! how thin and clear
    And thinner, clearer, farther going,
O sweet and far from cliff and seas
    The horns of Elfland faintly blowing!
Blow, let us hear the purple glens replying:
Blow, bugle; answer, echoes, dying, dying, dying.

O love, they die in yon rich sky
    They faint on hill or field or river;
Our echoes roll from soul to soul
    And grow for ever and for ever.
Blow, bugle, blow, set the wild echoes flying,
And answer, echoes, answer, dying, dying, dying.

Alfred, Lord Tennyson, 1809–92

ACKNOWLEDGEMENTS

There are some copyrights in this book which I could not trace. In recognition of this I have made a donation to the Royal Literary Fund, which helps needy authors. The publishers will be happy to rectify any omissions in future editions.

iii The Fledgling by John Anster Fitzgerald (1832–1906), The Maas Gallery, London/Bridgeman Art Library, London/New York **vi** The Reconciliation Oberon and Titania, 1847 by Sir Joseph Noel Paton (1821–1901), National Gallery of Scotland, Edinburgh/Bridgeman Art Library, London/New York **2** Midsummer Night's Dream by Sir Joseph Noel Paton (1821–1901), The Fine Art Society, London/Bridgeman Art Library, London/New York **5** A Glimpse of Fairies/Charles Lear (1818–1903), Fine Art Photographic Library Ltd **6** 'There Sleeps Titania', 1872 by John Simmons (1823–76), Private Collection/Bridgeman Art Library, London/New York **8** Midsummer Eve by Edward Robert Hughes (1851–1914), Fine Art Photographic Library Ltd **10** The Release of Ariel by John Anster Fitzgerald (1832–1906), Fine Art Photographic Library Ltd/Private Coll. **13** Asleep in the Moonlight by Richard Doyle (1824–83), British Library, London/Bridgeman Art Library, London/New York **16** Spirit of the Night by John Atkinson Grimshaw (1863–93), Fine Art Photographic Library Ltd/ Private Coll. **18** Thomas the Rhymer by Sir Joseph Noel Paton (1821–1901), Fine Art Photographic Library Ltd **20** Come Unto These Yellow Sands by Richard Dadd (1819–87), Fine Art Photographic Library Ltd **22** The Captive Robin by John Anster Fitzgerald (1832–1906), Christie's Images/Bridgeman Art Library, London/New York **25** Fairies' Whirl by Arthur John Black (1855–1936), Fine Art Photograhic Library Ltd **26** 'Who Killed Cock Robin?' by John Anster Fitzgerald (1832–1906), The Maas Gallery, London/Bridgeman Art Library, London/ New York **28** The Quarrel of Oberon and Titania, 1849 by Sir Joseph Noel Paton (1821–1901), National Gallery of Scotland, Edinburgh/Bridgeman Art Library, London/New York **31** Triumphal March of the Elf King by Richard Doyle (1824–83), British Library, London/Bridgeman Art Library, London/New York **32** The Haunted Park by Richard Doyle (1824–83), Fine Art Photographic Library Ltd/Private Coll. **35** There is Sweet Music Here by Charles Robinson (1870–1937), Angela Hone/Fine Art Photographic Library Ltd **36** The Concert by John Anster Fitzgerald (1832–1906), Fine Art Photographic Library/Private Coll. **38** Queen Mab from Shelley's poem by Henry Maynall Rheam (1859–1920), The Fine Art Society, London/Bridgeman Art Library, London/New York **40** The Fairy Queen – A Procession, 1882 (w/c) by Charles Altamont Doyle (1832–93), The Maas Gallery, London/Bridgeman Art Library, London/New York **43** Fairies, Anon. 19th century, Fine Art Photographic Library/Private Coll. **44** The Pixie's Meal by Rosa C. Petherick, Fine Art Photographic Library Ltd **45** The Faires' Banquet, 1859 by John Anster Fitzgerald (1832–1906), The Maas Gallery, London/Bridgeman Art Library, London/New York **47** Goblin Harvest, c. 1910 (w/c) by Amelia M. Bowerley or Bauerle (d. 1919) (attr. to), Private Collection/Bridgeman Art Library, London/New York **48** The Enchanted Forest by John Anster Fitzgerald (1832–1906), Fine Art Photographic Library Ltd **50** Midsummer Fairies, c. 1856 byJohn George Naish (1824–1905), Christopher Wood Gallery, London/Bridgeman Art Library, London/New York **52** The Marriage of Oberon and Titania by John Anster Fitzgerald (1832–1906), Private Collection/Bridgeman Art Library, London/New York **54** Friar Puck (oil on canvas) by Henry Fuseli (1741–1825), Tabley House Collection, University of Manchester/Bridgeman Art Library, London/New York **56** Puck, 1789 by Sir Joshua Reynolds (1732–92), Private Collection/Bridgeman Art Library, London/New York **57** Jack O'Lantern by Arthur Hughes (1832–1906), Christie's Images/Bridgeman Art Library, London/New York **59** Contradiction Oberon and Titania by Richard Dadd (1819–87), Fine Art Photographic Library Ltd **61** The Time I've Lost in Wooing by Daniel MacLise (1806–70), Fine Art Photographic Library Ltd **63** Faires in a Bird's Nest by John Anster Fitzgerald (1832–1906), The Maas Gallery, London/Bridgeman Art Library, London/ New York **67** Oberon and the Mermaid by SirJoseph Noel Paton (1821–1901), The Fine Art Society, London/Bridgeman Art Library, London/New York **68** Watching the Fairies, 1825 (w/c) by Beatrice Goldsmith (1895–1947), Chris Beetles Ltd, London/Bridgeman Art Library, London/New York **71** The Dance of the Little People by William Holmes Sullivan (d. 1908), Favin Graham Gallery/Fine Art Photographic Library Ltd **72** The Fairy Queen (oil on board) by Sir Joseph Noel Paton (1821–1947), Sheffield City Art Galleries/Bridgeman Art Library, London/New York **74** Titania by John Simmons (1823–76), Fine Art Photographic Library Ltd **77** The Haunt of the Fairies by Richard Dadd (1819–87), Forbes Magazine Collection, New York/Bridgeman Art Library, London/New York **78** The Enchanted Forest, 1886 (w/c) by Sir John Gilbert (1817–97), Guildhall Art Gallery, Corporation of London/ Bridgeman Art Library, London/New York **80** Hermia and Lysander by John Simmons (1823–76), Fine Art Photographic Library Ltd **82** Rabbit Among the Fairies by John Anster Fitzgerald (1832–1906), Fine Art Photographic Ltd **85** Once Upon a Time/Henry Maynall Rheam (1859–1920), Fine Art Photograhic Library Ltd/Private Coll. **87** The Lover's World by Eleanor Fortescue-Brickdale (1871–1945), City of Bristol Museum and Art Gallery/Bridgeman Art Library, London/New York **88** Titania by Frederick Howard Michael (d. 1936), Fine Art Photographic Library/Private Coll. **90** The Fairy Queen by Richard Painton (fl. c. 1921), Fine-Lines (Fine Art), Warwickshire/Bridgeman Art Library, London/New York **93** Titania, 1866 (w.c and gouache) by John Simmons (1832–1906),City of Bristol Museum and Art Gallery/Bridgeman Art Library, London/New York **95** The Fairy's Funeral by John Anster Fitzgerald (1832–1906), The Maas Gallery, London/ Bridgeman Art Library, London/New York **97** The Fairy Wood by Henry Maynell Rheam (1859–1920), Roy Miles Gallery, 29 Bruton Street, London W1/Bridgeman Art Library, London/ New York **101** What the Little Girl Saw in the Bush, 1904 by Frederck McCubbin (1855–1917), Private Collection/ Bridgeman Art Library, London/New York